D1613736

WATERLOO PUBLIC LIBRARY
33420013045720

Take a Closer Look at

The Internet

by JoAnn Early Macken

Content Consultant
William F. Pelgrin
Co-Founder
CyberWA, Inc.

RED
CHAIR
•PRESS• ™

Please visit our website at **www.redchairpress.com** for more high-quality products for young readers.

About the Author: JoAnn Early Macken has written more than 130 books for young readers. JoAnn earned her M.F.A. in Writing for Children and Young Adults at Vermont College of Fine Arts. She has taught writing at four Wisconsin colleges, and she speaks about poetry and writing to children and adults at schools, libraries, and conferences.

Publisher's Cataloging-In-Publication Data
Macken, JoAnn Early, 1953-
 Take a closer look at. The Internet / by JoAnn Early Macken ; content consultant, William F. Pelgrin, Past CEO, Center for Internet Security (CIS). -- [First edition].

 pages : illustrations, maps, charts ; cm

 Summary: Life would be very different without the Internet. Our governments depend on it. There would be no use for computers or mobile phones. Airlines would shut down. What can be done to safeguard the Internet? In this book, find out how scientists are working on ways to keep the Internet open and free from interruption. STEM career opportunities are featured. Includes a glossary and references for additional reading.
 "Core content library"--Cover.
 Interest age level: 006-010.
 Edition statement supplied by publisher.
 Issued also as an ebook. (ISBN: 978-1-63440-061-9)
 Includes bibliographical references and index.
 ISBN: 978-1-63440-053-4 (library hardcover)

 1. Internet--Social aspects--Juvenile literature. 2. Internet--Security measures--Juvenile literature. 3. Internet. 4. Internet--Security measures. I. Pelgrin, William F. II. Title. III. Title: Take a closer look at the Internet IV. Title: Internet

TK5105.875.I57 M33 2016
004.678

2015937990

Copyright © 2016 Red Chair Press LLC

All rights reserved. No part of this book may be reproduced, stored in an information or retrieval system, or transmitted in any form by any means, electronic, mechanical including photocopying, recording, or otherwise without the prior written permission from the Publisher. For permissions, contact info@redchairpress.com

Photo credits: Dreamstime: cover, 3, 11, 14, 25. Shutterstock: 3, 4, 5, 6, 7, 8, 9, 10, 11, 12, 13, 15, 17, 18, 19, 20, 21, 22, 23, 24, 25, 26, 27, 28, 29, 30, 31, 32, 33, 35, 36, 37, 38, 40

This series first published by:
Red Chair Press LLC   PO Box 333   South Egremont, MA 01258-0333

Printed in the United States of America
Distributed in the U.S. by Lerner Publisher Services. www.lernerbooks.com

112015 1P LPSS16

Contents

1 What is the Backround?

In 1958, a gallon of gas cost 25 cents. Elvis Presley crooned to his fans. That's when the first concept of the Internet began.

President Dwight D. Eisenhower took the first step. He started the Advanced Research Projects Agency, or ARPA. Its plan was to focus on technology. Computers were a big part of its mission. Back then, a computer could fill a whole room. It might cost a million dollars. Many users shared each one.

ARPA scientists had to work together. In 1969, they took a big leap. They linked four computers at four universities. They called the network **ARPANET** or **DARPANET** for Defense.

ARPANET users could search one computer with another one. They could copy files. They could send data.

The network grew in the 1970s. Soon other networks popped up. They linked together, too. This "inter-networking" became the Internet.

The Internet spread around the world. As it grew, it improved. Networks sped up. Computers worked faster. Computer companies created and sold smaller models. Over time computers were bought for both business and personal use.

Many early Internet users were scientists. Some were students. Others worked for the government. They all needed a simple system to find their way online. In 1991, they got one—the **World Wide Web**. It used **hypertext links** to connect web sites. And it was free! By then, the Internet linked nearly a million computers.

 Most early Internet users were scientists sharing data.

Navigating the Web

Soon web sites included more than text. They also used graphics, video, and sound. **Browsers** gave users a way to explore the Internet. **Search engines** helped them find what they were looking for.

Modern browsers include these and other features:

- main window to view web sites

- buttons to move back and forth between sites

- address bar, search bar, and status bar

- bookmarks and browsing history

- **HTML** source code view

- add-on programs for news, shopping, blogging, and more

Internet Touches Daily Life

Computer prices kept dropping. More and more people bought their own computer for use at home. Businesses built web sites to reach more customers. People could check the news, weather, and sports scores.

In the early 1990s, there were only about 600 web sites. But the online world kept growing. Amazon started selling books. The eBay auction site offered items for sale. PayPal gave people a way to pay for their orders. Newspapers started publishing on web sites. So did magazines. Blogs popped up. People expressed their own opinions. Music fans could listen to their favorite bands. They could buy music recordings from iTunes. They could shop. Plan travel routes. Book plane trips.

 iTunes changed how we listen to music.

Email changed how we communicate.

Email became an easy way to send messages—fast. And you could send mail to multiple people at one time. Time and distance did not matter any longer. You did not wait days and weeks for postal mail. Communication became immediate.

The World Wide Web Today

Now scientists share their research online. They read each other's results while tests are still going on. They build on other people's work instead of repeating it. Doctors consult with experts around the world. Patients read their own charts. Find test results and ask questions.

The Internet lets doctors share medical records.

Workers can do many jobs from home. They share documents. They link to office files. They even see each other in video meetings. Friends visit with each other online, too. Travelers chat with their families at home. College students check in with their parents. Grandparents read books to their grandchildren with video services such as Skype.

Many schools offer classes online. Museums show exhibit details. Zoos share animal facts and videos with the community. Real estate companies show property for sale. Banks offer bill paying and other services online. Readers search library catalogs. They find and reserve books. They may even borrow digital Ebooks.

Shoppers compare prices online. They look up everything from shoes to canoes. People with places to go request rides and pay for them online.

Today, people watch TV and movies online. Play games, alone or with others. Film their own videos and post them on YouTube. They show how to fix a flat tire or make maple syrup. They show pets doing silly tricks. Some videos are just to make people laugh.

Web cams show wildlife in their own habitats. Organizations raise funds for good causes. Politicians reach out to voters. Activists create petitions, and people sign them online.

On social media sites, people find and socialize with former classmates and friends. Social media lets people follow the antics of celebrities. Stay in touch with relatives and friends.

Our Changing World

The Internet has helped create jobs unheard of a generation ago. Programmers. Web designers. Help desk workers. Online sales forces. Order fillers.

Cyber cafes cater to Internet users. Hotels and coffee shops offer free **Wi-Fi**. Even airplanes have Internet access.

People link to the Internet with smart phones. Tablet computers. Watches. Even toys are connected. And the Internet keeps growing.

★ Free Wi-Fi is not secure. Never share personal information.

★ Internet devices are smaller and smaller.

Amazon Changes Things

Amazon began in 1995 as a web site selling only books. They now sell almost anything. In 2015, the company employed more than 150,000 people in over 130 locations around the world.

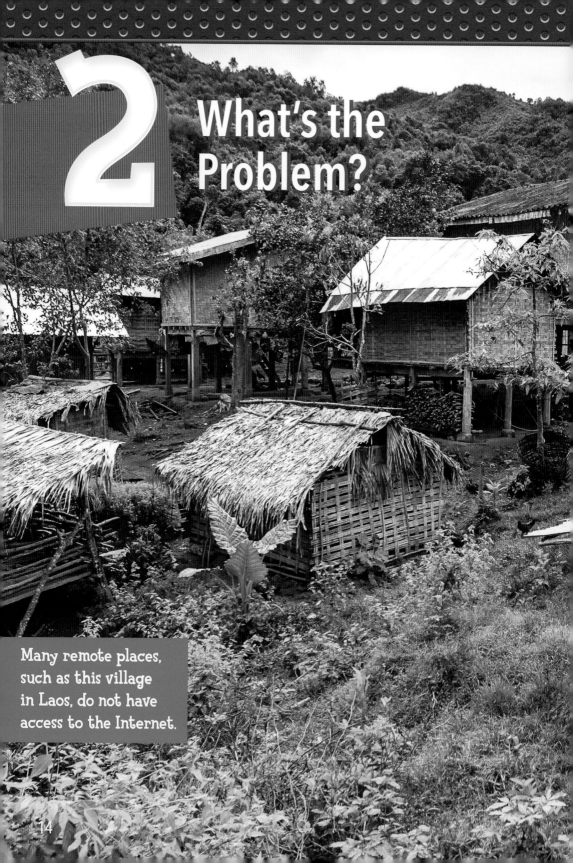

2 What's the Problem?

Many remote places, such as this village in Laos, do not have access to the Internet.

Not everyone benefits from the Internet. Many people do not own computers. They might be able to use one at a public library. But their access is limited. Who is left behind? People with low incomes. People whose internet service is slow or not reliable. People who live in places with no access. In 2014, that was nearly 60% of the world.

Confusing Technology

Internet technology is still new. It can confuse users. They might change a setting by accident. Then they don't know how to undo the change. Some schools teach students how to use computers and software. Other people might have to figure out how to use the technology on their own. They might not be able to find help online. Even if they do, it's not always current or user friendly.

True or False

Web sites are only as helpful as their content. Many are not kept current. Outdated information can be misleading or wrong. Users waste time because of broken links for long-gone pages.

On the Internet, anyone can pose as an expert. Anyone can spread false information. Do you want to use a web site for research? Be sure it's reliable first. Check with your parent or teacher as to web sites you can trust. Web sites like Wikipedia are useful for quick information. But because it is open to anyone to post updates to the information, it is not always accurate.

★ **Some web sites are designed with kids in mind.**

Scams, Spam, and Viruses

Scammers often prey on people who don't recognize a threat. An email scam, known as **phishing**, might ask for help. It offers free money. In exchange, it asks for bank account details.

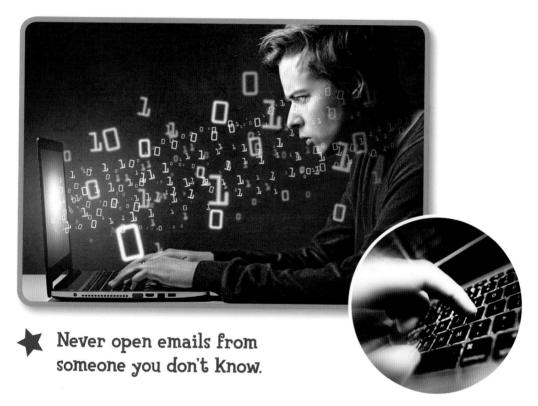

⭐ Never open emails from someone you don't know.

An email, for example, is sent with a real company name. But it comes from a fake address. It may ask people for their passwords or other personal information.

A thief can use this information. Empty victims' bank accounts. Steal their identities.

Junk email, or **spam**, is usually sent to to many addresses at once. Some of it is harmless. Some is dangerous.

An email can contain a virus. The virus can infect users' computers. It might cause real damage. It might even make a computer useless.

Viruses make copies of themselves. Over and over. They spread to other computers. A web site can spread a virus, too. A user clicks a link that promises a free book. The link may send a virus instead.

Antivirus programs combat viruses. **Firewalls** may block them. But new viruses keep popping up.

Cyber Crime

Cyber criminals use computers for illegal acts. **Hackers** break into computers or networks. They read other people's email. Some email programs **encrypt** messages, or put them in code. That makes them harder for hackers to read. Hackers can install spyware. It records what users do. They can steal passwords. Health records. Credit card numbers and Social Security Numbers. That data can lead to identity theft.

BE CYBER SAFE

1. Never tell anyone other than a parent or guardian your passwords, not even your best friend.

2. Never use your own name as a username or a picture of yourself for your avatar.

3. If someone asks you to send information on where you live, or what activities you do, don't answer, and tell an adult.

4. Never use a camera or voice chat while playing online games with strangers.

5. The size of your social network is not a competition. Don't accept 'friend' requests from people you don't know.

Backlash and Bullying

On a social media site, anyone can create a fake profile. Anyone can pretend to be a friend. Predators prey on the unwary. Even children can be victims.

A comment meant to be private can spread. You should never write mean or cruel comments online. And you should never respond to comments meant to hurt your feelings online.

Online bullying is a concern for many kids and parents. Victims need a safe way to speak up.

 You should always tell an adult if you are the victim of cyber-bullying.

Nothing is Private Online

It can be fun to take photos with friends, but once a picture is sent via email or SMS, the photo is out of your control. Your photos and 'selfies' can be posted on social media without your knowledge for anyone to see.

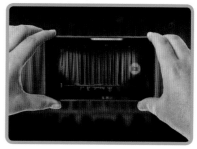

★ Recording movies or performances may be illegal.

Online Pirates

Books, music, and movies are all available online now. But writers, musicians, and filmmakers are not always paid for their work. Pirates make illegal copies and sell them. They take income from the artists.

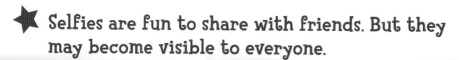

★ Selfies are fun to share with friends. But they may become visible to everyone.

3 Are We Too Connected?

These days, one tweet or blog post can reach millions of readers. We've gained a huge audience for our thoughts. We've gained instant readers and responses. We've also gained a constant input of messages. Some are important. Others are meaningless.

People on cell phones walk their dogs or babies in strollers. People in restaurants stare at their phones. Do they see the people they share a meal with? Do they taste their food? Being always connected might mean losing touch with whoever and whatever is right in front of us.

Things have changed so fast we can hardly keep up. But many of us keep trying. We might be better off if we realized we can't.

Getting Personal

In spite of all the online opportunities, what have we lost? Perhaps one-to-one contact. How could we find it again? Unplug once in a while and talk to your friends and family.

23

Before the Internet, people wrote long, newsy letters. They chose fancy stationery. They wrote with their favorite pens. They walked to the corner, dropped the letters in a mailbox, and waited for the mail carrier to bring a reply.

Those days are over. But many people still enjoy taking the time to craft a personal message. Many people love to receive letters and cards, too. Why not write to someone special? Send a Thank You note. Send a postcard from a vacation spot. Send a personal drawing to an older relative.

Before the Internet, families watched their favorite TV shows together. They played cards or board games. They worked on jigsaw puzzles.

Go Outside!

What else could you do? Take a walk.
Get involved in sports. Volunteer.
Visit people. Learn to identify trees or
insects or birds. Ride a bike. Play soccer.
Journal. Paint, draw or play music. Watch a play
or a movie in a theater. Slow down and pay attention.
Be more well-rounded! It's good for a healthy life.

4 Where Do We Go From Here?

The Internet keeps evolving. What does the future hold? Some predictions sound like science fiction. So did the idea of the Internet not long ago.

The Internet of Things

More devices will connect to to the Internet and to each other. New devices inspire new uses. New uses inspire new devices. How many things link to the Internet now? One company's estimate is 15 billion. That's more than the number of people on Earth! And the number keeps going up. By 2020, they say, it could be 50 billion. New types of devices will connect, too. Cars. Refrigerators. Parking meters. Thermostats. Heart monitors. Devices that haven't been invented yet.

To provide access for new devices, providers are looking up to the sky. Satellite networks are expensive. They might use drones or balloons instead.

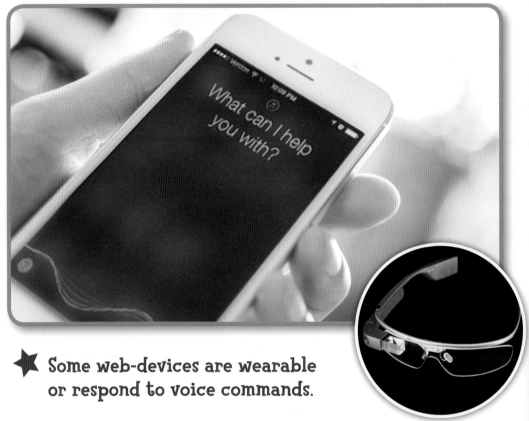

★ Some web-devices are wearable or respond to voice commands.

Size and Power

What will power all these devices? In the future, maybe the human body. Running could provide energy. Walking could recharge a cell phone.

Computers will keep shrinking. Someday, we might wear them. People wear smart glasses now. They can include cameras. GPS systems. Buttons control some types. Some kinds follow head or arm motions. Others use voice commands. Speech recognition software keeps improving. It even translates speech. It could help people who have disabilities.

Wearable devices keep getting smaller. Some of them, such as pace-makers, fit inside our bodies. They could check vital signs. They might help detect cancer or heart problems. Contact lenses could help monitor our health.

Computers will surely be more powerful. **Artificial Intelligence** (AI) could help machines learn. Robots already work on farms. They could help in hospitals. Computers could be as smart as people. Someday, perhaps, even smarter.

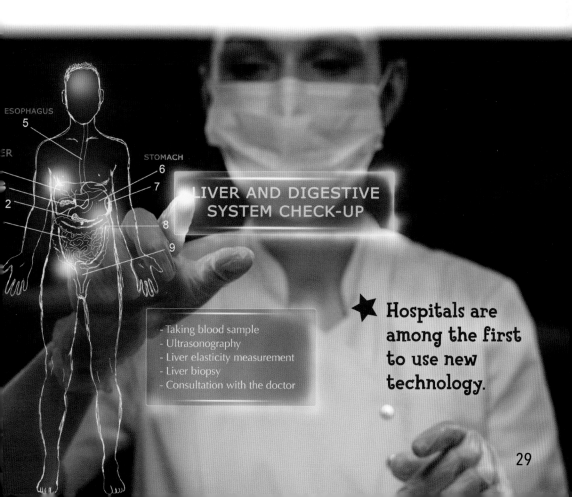

ESOPHAGUS
5

ER

STOMACH
6

7

2

8

9

LIVER AND DIGESTIVE SYSTEM CHECK-UP

- Taking blood sample
- Ultrasonography
- Liver elasticity measurement
- Liver biopsy
- Consultation with the doctor

★ Hospitals are among the first to use new technology.

Smarter Systems

With more data, things run better. Businesses can keep fewer items in stock. Smart cities can control traffic. A bridge might send an alarm if it needs repair. Smart farming could help farmers grow more and waste less. Cars could drive themselves.

Some of these systems are already in place. People can control their home heat and lights from a distance. Smart forests measure changes in the environment. That helps scientists keep track of climate change.

★ Cars that park themselves and brake before accidents, are being tested now.

★ The Internet lets some people lock doors and control lights at home from their phones.

Computers play a huge role in the military. Encrypted messages help prevent spying. Software can locate enemy shooters. Training is based on video games.

Scientists are already working on an Internet in space. It is designed to connect Earth to the International Space Station. Perhaps it could also listen for signals from other life forms.

Knowledge and Power

Managing the Internet keeps getting harder. A core group of designers works on its structure. That group keeps growing. More people have an interest in how the Internet works. More businesses rely on it for profits. More workers rely on it for jobs. More users rely on it for entertainment. They all have a stake in its future.

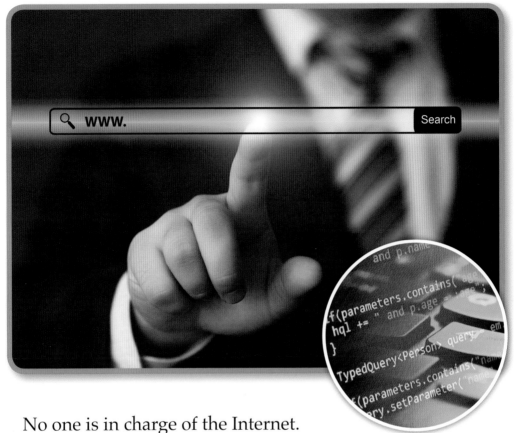

No one is in charge of the Internet. But some governments try to control it. They try to spy on users. Those efforts can lead to loss of privacy. Leading to censorship and oppression.

One key choice shaped the Internet. All users should have equal, open access. It should benefit everyone. **Net Neutrality** means that everyone's data is treated the same. No users should receive better service than others. Not even for a higher price.

Access is still an issue in many places. We must keep improving it. We need to invest to be sure everyone has reliable service.

The Digital Divide

The Internet must be available to all. If not, it could be one more way to divide rich from poor. The **digital divide** is the gap between those who have access to information and technology and those who do not. It is still too wide in many places, including the United States.

The number of Internet users keeps rising. About 84% of the people in the United States had access in 2014. Across the globe, the number is only about 44%. Here are figures from some other countries.

Countries with Lowest % Internet Access	% Access	Countries with Highest % Internet Access	% Access
Eritrea	0.90	Luxembourg	93.78
Timor-Leste	1.10	Liechtenstein	93.80
Myanmar	1.20	Netherlands	93.96
Burundi	1.30	Andorra	94.00
Somalia	1.50	Denmark	94.63
Guinea	1.60	Sweden	94.78
Niger	1.70	Norway	95.05
Sierra Leone	1.70	Bermuda	95.30
Ethiopia	1.90	Iceland	96.55
Congo (Dem. Rep.)	2.20	Falkland (Malvinas) Is.	96.90

Source: International Telecommunication Union, 2014 report

The Internet affects our lives in huge ways. Without it, we'd miss a lot. It's safe to say that the Internet will be a force in the world for some time to come.

Using It Wisely

The Internet gives us a wealth of knowledge. We could learn more by reading the opinions of others. Expand your horizons. Learn about life in other parts of the world. That could bring us all closer together. Make the best use of this huge, valuable resource!

STEM Career Connections

All over the world, workers are needed in four key areas:

- Science
- Technology
- Engineering
- Math

Scientists work in research labs. They also go out in the world to observe. They collect data to study.

Technology puts science to practical use. Many STEM jobs are related to computers.

Engineers solve problems. They invent and design new products.

Math is a key skill in many kinds of jobs such as video game designers.

The Internet keeps growing. It will need trained workers for some time to come. They'll use math to figure out costs. They'll study science data. Think up new theories. Explore safer methods. Document systems. Repair broken devices. They might focus on these and other issues:

- providing equal access to everyone
- decreasing computer size and increasing power
- cyber security for users

STEM skills help people working with the Internet in these fields.

- aerospace
- biotechnology
- education
- energy
- entertainment
- environment
- health care
- manufacturing
- research and development
- sales and marketing
- transportation

How will the Internet fit into your future?

Resources

Books

Avoiding Online Hoaxes (Cyberspace Survival Guide) by Therese M. Shea. Gareth Stevens Publishing (2012)

Combating Computer Viruses (Cyberspace Survival Guide) by John M. Shea. Gareth Stevens Publishing (2012)

Dealing with Cyberbullies (Cyberspace Survival Guide) by Drew Nelson. Gareth Stevens Publishing (2012)

Internet Safety (Let's Read and Talk About) by Anne Rooney. Sea to Sea Publications (2013)

Social Networking and Social Media Safety (Stay Safe Online) by Eric Minton. Powerkids Press (2014)

Web Sites and Videos

Online Bullying:
http://pbskids.org/itsmylife/friends/bullies/article8.html

Safe Cyberspace Surfing: http://kidshealth.org/kid/watch/house/internet_safety.html?tracking=K_RelatedArticle

Safe Search Kids child friendly search engine powered by Google: http://kidshealth.org/kid/watch/house/internet_safety.html

What is the world wide web?
http://www.bbc.co.uk/guides/z2nbgk7

Glossary

ARPANET: a group of computers linked together by ARPA, the Advanced Research Projects Agency. Often called DARPANET (D:Defense).

Artificial Intelligence (AI): the intelligence of machines or software

browser: a software program that enables users to navigate within and between web sites

digital divide: gap between those who have access to technology and data and those who do not

encrypt: to put into code

firewall: a software program or piece of hardware that helps screen out hackers, viruses, and worms that try to reach your computer over the Internet

hacker: a person who breaks into a computer or network

HTML: HyperText Markup Language, language used to create web pages

hypertext link: a piece of computer code that links one site to another. Clicking a mouse accesses a link.

Net Neutrality: the concept that everyone's date is treated the same way on the Internet

phishing: a scam that attempts to steal personal information by posing as a legitimate company or person asking for accounts, passwords, etc.

search engine: software that searches for information on the World Wide Web

spam: junk email, often sent to many addresses at once

Wi-Fi: wireless networking technology that connects to the Internet with radio waves

World Wide Web: system of linked documents accessed by the Internet

Index